CHINESE-AMERICAN INTERACTIONS:
A Historical Summary

The 1974 Brown and Haley Lectures are the twenty-first of a series that has been given annually at the University of Puget Sound, Tacoma, Washington, by a scholar distinguished for work in the Social Studies or Humanities. The purpose of these lectures is to present original analyses of some intellectual problems confronting the present age.

JOHN K. FAIRBANK

CHINESE-AMERICAN INTERACTIONS:

A Historical Summary

RUTGERS UNIVERSITY PRESS

New Brunswick, New Jersey

Library of Congress Cataloging in Publication Data

Fairbank, John King, 1907–
  Chinese-American interactions.

  (The Brown & Haley lectures; 1974)
  Bibliography: p.
  1. United States—Foreign relations—China—
Addresses, essays, lectures. 2. China—Foreign
relations—United States—Addresses, essays, lectures.
I. Title. II. Series.
E183.8.C5F29   301.29′51′073   74-22192
ISBN 0-8135-0784-7
ISBN 0-8135-0785-5 pbk

CONTENTS

FOR DOROTHY BORG

CHINESE-AMERICAN INTERACTIONS:
A *Historical Summary*

INTRODUCTION

Twenty years ago historians studied the Western impact on China—all those nineteenth-century activities that brought opium, Christian tracts, modern inventions, and ideas like nationalism into that ancient civilization. Today there is also a Chinese impact on the United States. Material technology is still flowing mainly one way, toward China, except for Chinese discoveries like acupuncture anesthesia; but administrative and social ideas are another matter. Chairman Mao professes to need nothing of the sort from us save as a horrible example. But many Americans are interested in Chinese methods of political mobilization, child-rearing and education, low-cost health care, family planning, and keeping ecological balance on the land. These are matters of large-scale but decentralized organization; they have been a Chinese specialty for many centuries. Today the Chinese genius for social order is being newly applied to the problems of national development on the supermassive scale that only China can provide.

For Americans generally, however, the contemporary Chinese impact is probably strongest in historical studies. The American view of mankind is being rounded out, and Chinese history is becoming a necessary part of our curriculum.

The study of China as another society and culture has been a major focus for interdisciplinary area studies in the United States during the last three decades, ever since area study got its primal impetus in World War II. Chinese studies have required the social sciences to be used in historical depth, a lesson that derives particularly from the study of another society. Taking the social sciences as efforts to be scientific about human life together, just as the earlier natural sciences had been scientific about nature, we have come upon the fact that a society is less like a machine than like a person, existing through time and with a history. Applying the social sciences to the alien society of China inevitably points up the need for historical knowledge—for a four-dimensional approach through time rather than a behaviorial approach in the present moment only. In practice this means that a broader grasp of Chinese institutions, thought, and literature is bringing us to a new level of competence in our reach toward a social-science analysis of Chinese ways of behavior.

This analysis is urgently needed, to judge by our errors in understanding during the last generation. The top United States decision makers, not being sinologists, have had to make do with our common public knowledge of East Asia. In this respect they have been truly representative of the profound public ignorance. Pearl Harbor, for example, was a great surprise to everyone on this side of the world, quite beyond the American anticipation of events.

In 1950 General MacArthur, having checked the North Korean invasion of South Korea, started for the Yalu River to unify the country. It didn't work out that way. We were again severely defeated. In retrospect we can see that the Chinese simply had to come into the war—as they had said they were going to do—because the Yalu was on the border of their main industrial region. MacArthur and the Joint Chiefs had overlooked basic facts.

Then in the 1950's we got into the great monolithic-international-communist misconception. We decided that because the Soviet Union and Stalin in particular said that international communism was a monolith, therefore it was, and the Chinese were part of it. It took us ten years to begin to recognize that the Chinese really were not going to stick with the Russians, as could have been foreseen, I think, if enough historical knowledge and thought had been applied to the subject. It took us still another twelve years to act on the reality. As of 1960, the Sino-Soviet split was fully apparent. Only twelve years later Mr. Nixon got to his rapprochement, a little slow for modern times. We can't wait that long to do the obvious thing. The minute the Sino-Soviet split appeared, it created a triangular politics that we were bound to participate in sooner or later.

This brings us to the sad subject of Vietnam. There it is fairly plain that the United States acted from a vacuum of knowledge, and so from a great distance we imposed our own images and stereotypes on the scene, quite inappropriately. The most glaring missing ingredient in

American policy in Vietnam was any appreciation of Vietnamese history. I sympathize with the policy makers on this point, because until I went there in 1960, I had not fully understood that Vietnam existed as part of the ancient Chinese culture area. If I as an individual working on China was in this benighted condition, how can I blame anybody else? I don't, but it is a fact that we were ignorant of Vietnamese history. If we had known a little, we would have known that Vietnam is a country older than France, with a longer recorded history, and that it has generally been expanding throughout the last millennium of its history from north to south. For the last thousand years it has also been independent of China, though tributary, and it has repulsed Chinese invasions on several occasions.

All of this is after-spilt-milk, of course. We can conclude that American intellectual inertia is a dangerous hindrance in dealing with East Asia, a region that we don't know much about from our own past, and this is translated into institutional inertia, which is also dangerous. After all, it has taken fourteen years at Harvard to promote a chair in Vietnamese history. We began in 1960, and only now are we within sight of having this post created and filled. There has been a grievous, long-drawn-out war in the meantime, and no end of trouble affecting all the world. Yet even today few other American universities have posts in Vietnamese history. Lest I seem to extol Harvard, let me report that only recently have Vietnamese books in the modern vernacular been accepted in its Chinese-Japanese Library as part of the necessary equipment of East Asian studies; yet Harvard claims to be a leader in this field. Let me avoid throwing stones for fear of getting hit, and merely suggest that present prospects for the future of Chinese-American relations are grim. We Americans will have to do a lot better in our approach to the Chinese if we expect to escape serious disasters some years hence.

This book is entitled *Chinese-American Interactions*, and certain assumptions are implicit in this title, of which you should be forewarned. The first is that a meeting of cultures is at issue. The two societies can be rather simply characterized: on the American side, as one that stresses individual enterprise, which is expansive; and on the Chinese side, as a society that stresses the collective social order, which is resistant.

The assumption that we should treat China as a culture, a civilization, an entity, is implicit in Chinese thinking about China. Among scholars, this assumption is rapidly breaking down, as people look at the bits and pieces and see that China is composed of many different things. Nevertheless, at this stage of our understanding, there is no question that China presents itself to us as an entity, a civilization. First it has been separate in space, faraway in East Asia, its interior largely inaccessible from the earliest times. Few Europeans could get across the high deserts and river valley jungles of Asia to reach it. The journey by sea was also long and hazardous. There wasn't much contact. Second, China is both ancient and continuous in time, with a long historical record. Third, it has been for the most part self-contained. It has not needed much from the outside. Fourth, it is the biggest polity that has ever been seen—in the sheer number of people. The mass and inertia of this body politic still present a problem—how might it be deflected from any course it pursues? I don't think it can be. China is the original center of the East Asian civilization, which spread out from the mainland around the fringes. Nowadays the East Asian coastal fringe includes Japan, South Korea, southern Vietnam, and Taiwan, a province of China. These places are all in the international trading order to which America and Europe belong. China, however, remains separate from this trading order. It is not nearly so dependent on trade as most other countries. It is still a self-sufficient, vast society going its own way.

This has led the China-specialist tribe first to think of Chinese culture as separate, distinctive, and different, and then to expatiate on the differences. This is the old stock-in-trade of the China specialist ever since Marco Polo: everything in China is upside down, and so forth. The opposite to the assumption of China's peculiar cultural entity is of course natural to social scientists and also to Marxists: China may be different, but it still is a human society, and humankind, as studied through the social sciences, has similar characteristics around the world. Marxists assume that the stages of historical change in China will be the same as anywhere else, feudal, bourgeois, socialist. . . . Yet thoughts of China's uniqueness as a culture and its common traits with other societies are not inconsistent. One of the first things to do in trying to understand China is to hold in mind inconsistent and incompatible ideas.

Another assumption is that the stimulus for the traveler is always greater than for the fellow who stays at home and gets his notions of foreign parts from reading or hearsay. In the early days Americans who went to China received a tremendous impact. They wrote home about it and came home to talk about it. Similarly, in the later period when a Chinese student went abroad, he received a great impact from the strange places and people he visited, and he took back various impressions of his Western experience. This mutual impact is immensely interesting. Perhaps we can assume that in the early days the cumulative experience of the missionary had a greater effect on the United States than on China; only later did the missionary have more influence in China.

Other characteristics that becloud international understanding are the fluctuation of images and the ambivalence that each society sees in the other. Take, for example, the good China that Americans have seen in Charlie Chan, and the bad China in Dr. Fu Manchu. There are two faces to the other party. Sometimes he is a menace, at other times he is a good guy and the subject of a great deal of idealization. We Americans switch back and forth between these stereotypes. Evidently we are a volatile people. After we have hated or feared somebody for a while, we tire of this attitude and are glad to love him for a while; yet we tire of that, too, and are likely to shift round again. In developing stereotypes about China, we have tended to support the good guys, as we conceive them, against the bad guys. Meantime, we have always had a hope for trade, believing that with so many people, if China just would open its market, we could make enormous sales, but this never has happened. Strategically, we have had a tendency to oppose any power that seemed likely to dominate the East Asian continent, just as in Europe we have opposed anybody who, like Napoleon or Hitler, seemed likely to dominate that continent.

The Chinese on their side developed a whole series of responses and stereotypes in their contact with Americans. They began by seeking to defend themselves in the nineteenth century, and trying to get the guns, ships, and arsenals to do it with. Very soon they were led to a second step, aware that to produce arms, industry was essential, including transport and factories, textiles and other things useful against economic invasion. And finally, out of this contact came feelings of nationalism, which led China into reform and revolution.

I

MERCHANTS AND MISSIONARIES: BEGINNINGS AND FRUSTRATIONS TO THE 1870's

Let us look at the early American traders and evangelists who went to China, then consider both the early Chinese view of the Americans and the early American view of the Chinese.*

The Americans of the late eighteenth century had a very special view of the world, together with a self-image that is hard for us to remember now, even though we have inherited from it certain reflex reactions. The Americans believed that they had a special message for mankind, that they were a new breed of people, new compared with the Europeans. They believed in egalitarian democracy. They believed in small government, government that would help the enterprise of the individual and not hinder him, give him protection when necessary. They believed

* This overview is inspired by the work of a great many people whose writing represents a national explosion of interest in trying to understand the East Asian part of our horizon, which is in fact our western trans-Pacific horizon. See the bibliographical note at end of text.

that their free enterprise promised a superior way of life both materially and spiritually, vastly better than the old societies of Europe or the British empire or any other empire they might come up against.

With these beliefs, the Americans were very expansive. Undoubtedly, they were also self-righteous. Abroad, they must have annoyed many people, quite as much as they do today. They expanded by land in the westward movement, so fabled in song and story and every American history course. The westward movement, we are told, formed us. It is seldom noted that there was also an eastward movement by sea and that this was at the outset greater than the westward movement across this continent. The movement by sea reached around the world for trade—to the Mediterranean and around the Cape of Good Hope into the Indian Ocean and finally to the Far East. This trade was necessary to the young republic in its beginnings as a small Atlantic power kept out of the West Indies by the British empire.

The Americans who set out for the Near East were of three kinds. First to arrive was the merchant, who tried out what he could do on foreign shores, and then, particularly if the merchant got in trouble, the naval diplomat, a captain or a commodore with a warship who provided a little gunboat diplomacy to help out the merchant. The missionary followed along behind, seizing the opportunity to try to improve the local people's spiritual welfare.

This combination began on the Barbary Coast. The United States Navy was created mainly because the "Barbary pirates," the rulers of the Islamic North African states, were seizing American vessels, holding them for ransom, and sequestering their cargoes. The Navy was

built to protect this trade by police action, and so we
became accustomed to acting as self-appointed agents of
the international trading society. Many of the naval officers who operated on the Barbary Coast made their fame
there, then turned up in the Far East twenty or thirty years
later. Commodore Perry, for instance, came into promi-
nence when he opened Japan in 1854, but he had begun as
a "powder and ball" expert on the Barbary Coast in the
1820's. There were several others like him. The merchant,
the missionary, and the naval diplomat each pursued individual ends abroad, but they also helped each other.
Their Mediterranean experience was the prototype for
their later China experience.

What picture emerges from the writings left by one
person after another who engaged in the China trade?
These were typically young men aged about seventeen or
eighteen, who sailed from Boston, Salem, or Marblehead,
or from Baltimore or Philadelphia, and reached the coast
of China. A young American out on this great adventure
across the sea, having survived all the perils of storm and
shipwreck in a small vessel, on reaching the coast of China
sees first a Chinese junk, a sailing vessel with a different
hull, different rig, with lateen sails and eyes painted on
the bow—quite exotic, quite strange. And then entering
the Canton estuary, he picks up a pilot, a genuine Chinese
of distinctive features and dress, who boards from a sam-
pan and takes the American vessel into port, through the
Hu-men (Tiger's gate or Boca Tigris), which is flanked by
the two impressive promontories at the mouth of the Pearl
River. Having made this passage up the river with the
pilot, he meets little boats that come alongside to sell
things, the exoticism mounts, and finally he gets to

Whampoa. This is the sailors' port, the anchorage some twelve miles below the city of Canton. There he finds exoticism really commercialized. Samshu (rice wine) is available for the sailor, plus singsong girls and all sorts of things.

From Whampoa he goes by a smaller boat up to the Thirteen Factories at Canton. The Factories are again subjects of much legend. They are a sort of ghetto, a golden ghetto because the foreign merchants can make a good deal of money there. If the American boy doesn't die of fever, he may go home with a fortune in a few years. The Factories are a special place set aside for foreigners, who are given the opportunity to come to China and fit into their assigned role, or else stay away.

Many Americans who had this experience of Canton left a record of it in memoirs and letters home, and so helped create the adventurous mystique that surrounds the old China trade.

In Canton, the Americans found that they were in an Anglo-Saxon community, and that they had a lot in common with the British. They not only spoke the same language and worshiped the same Protestant God but perceived that all the foreigners together represented Christendom and progress. The Americans found Englishmen in Canton who were also private traders even before 1834, while the East India Company still had its monopoly of British trade. The Anglo-American private traders were individualist adventurers out to see what they could make in trade through their own ingenuity.

Like the British in the Canton community, the Americans coped with the problem of laying down funds in China in order to buy teas and silks for the Western markets. For this the Americans went to their northwest coast, typically to Puget Sound, to get sea otter skins and furs. They also stopped at the Sandwich Islands, now known as Hawaii, to get sandalwood. They also found some ginseng root in the hills of Oregon and Washington. It was of rather low quality, but they could get it from the Indians and take it to China where it would have high value. Ginseng root is supposed even today to have great medicinal or restorative properties, especially for aging males. Therefore it commanded a high price.

Out of the need for something to take to China, the traders soon hit upon the fact that opium was a useful commodity. The opium trade began at the end of the eighteenth century. The Americans couldn't go to India for their cargo, for here the British raj was permitting extensive opium production and letting the private British take it to China. The Americans could only go to Turkey. The supply was small, but still it was opium and the Chinese would buy it. The Smyrna opium trade was begun by a certain Mr. Wilcox of Philadelphia in 1804, but it was best organized by the Boston merchants, who in that period really were the most Yankee merchants of all. As the American China trade built up, the opium component became very useful, not as essential as it was to the revenues of British India but quite useful nevertheless.

In this way still another implicit assumption became established: that the American and other Western traders in China were not responsible for the welfare of that heathen and backward kingdom. The Chinese would have to look out for themselves; and if they would persist in buying and smuggling opium, that was their problem, not the foreigners'.

The main Boston firm, Russell and Company, had an interlocking directorship of first families. The names that were listed as partners of Russell and Company were also prominent along Brattle Street or in the Harvard Corporation—Forbes, Perkins, Russell, Cushing, Cunningham, Sturgis, Griswold, Delano, Bryant, Cabot, Paine, Higginson, Alsop. An offshoot of Russell, Augustine Heard and Company, included Coolidges. These leading citizens of the leading China trade city led as best they could both in the opium trade and in the tea trade. Particularly during the Opium War of 1840–1842, while the British were fighting, the Americans remained neutral, and this was very convenient both for the Americans and for the British, because the Americans as neutrals carried the British cargoes in and out of China.

The opium trade was a quick money-maker, but by the middle of the nineteenth century, although it could still be a source of profit, it was of less value for investment. That is, it wasn't something an American could stay with and build up. The American Middle West was opening up, and so leaders in Russell and Company, like John Murray Forbes, pulled out of the China trade in the 1840's and became railway organizers. Later, in the 1850's, other merchants of the China trade began to come back with funds and go into railways. Boston China merchants went into the Middle West. John Murray Forbes organized the Michigan Central in the 1850's, and then he put together the CB & Q—Chicago, Burlington & Quincy—one of the first big combinations of short railways all strung together. In short, if you could trade successfully in China, you could do even better in the United States.

The China trade in the first half of the nineteenth

century was an important source of capital accumulated for America's domestic development thereafter. Indeed, the great friend of Russell and Company, the Canton hong merchant Howqua, invested in the CB & Q, and so Chinese money went to work in the American Middle West.

Thus American traders made a strong beginning in the newly opened Chinese treaty ports. In the 1850's Americans had been the first to develop the clipper ship, to carry cargoes faster. When Britain repealed the navigation laws that had kept foreign trading vessels out of British colonies and home waters, the Americans had their chance. Their shipping forged ahead since they could now carry teas and silks and china to England. Americans in Shanghai became leaders of the foreign community along with the British. They were almost as numerous and very enterprising. Edward Cunningham of Russell and Company went into business with local Chinese and with the Shanghai taotai Wu Chien-chang, who had special insider's opportunities. The Sino-American cooperation that American merchants could work out in the treaty ports had various rewards. When the Salem adventurer Frederick Townsend Ward turned up in Shanghai in 1860 and began to lead a small mercenary force to protect the city against the Taiping rebels, he was financed by the merchant Yang Fang. Ward married Yang's daughter, renounced his American citizenship, and was appointed a Chinese military officer and paid by the Chinese government.

Yet the Civil War marked more or less the end of the old China trade. The Civil War years disrupted trading activities, but apart from that, the Americans turned inward. The development of their own country presented a greater opportunity than anything they could do in China.

And what of the missionary as a counterpart of the merchant in this early period? What was he doing in his separate approach to China?

Missionaries, of course, have been decried in recent years as "cultural imperialists." This may be accepted if one assumes that anything should be called imperialist that comes from abroad and is not liked in retrospect, as is frequently the case in revolutionary China. The missionary was intellectually aggressive and is today resented for having been so. In fact, the missionary had a high visibility, always working among the Chinese population, seeking converts, and building his church institutions, chapels, schools, and hospitals. He might be called the forerunner of latter-day aid programs.

Missionaries became the chief foreign presence in the interior of China outside the treaty ports and were always helpful to the foreign traveler. When my wife and I were traveling in Shansi province in 1935, we came to the walled city of Chao-ch'eng, one of the ancient local capitals of Shansi. We asked for any foreigners there, and were led to the house of the C.I.M. (China Inland Mission) missionary, Mr. Tuckey. Tuckey had been the name of my scout at Oxford, where I had had the privilege of being an upper-class person. A foreign scholar in England in the late 1920's became a member of the upper class by being in the university; so I knew the distinction between upper class and lower class, as I might not have known about it in my home state of South Dakota. Tuckey is a cockney name. My scout at Balliol College, who practically ran my life for me, was named Tuckey. And here was a Mr. Tuckey in Shansi province. He had come from the lower classes, as did most missionaries from England, and in a Maughamesque way he maintained his cultural ties with home by getting in Cross and Blackwell marmalade at considerable expense, though he had good oranges locally, and he also got the *Times*, which came in big bundles once a month. He would open the bundle, put the earliest date on top, and every day take off a copy of the *Times* and read it while having his toast and marmalade. A cultural extrusion maintaining his tenuous contact with home, he would be back in England for a bit, and then come back to work in Shansi.

It is a question today whether we can grasp the evangelical spirit of the American missionary expansion of the early 1800's. Good Christians not only believed all the things in the Bible in rather literal terms, including hell and damnation; many of them also believed that the millennium was about to come, the Day of Judgment when Christ would reappear. Such was a mentality we can not easily appreciate today. In the Second Great Awakening of the early nineteenth century, the revival movement in New England was closely connected with that in England. Evangelists built up their tract and Bible societies the better to spread the Word. They developed a periodical press. They supported humanitarian causes in the spirit of "disinterested benevolence" and were against the slave trade and similar evils. Since the United States, after all, was smaller than Britain at the time (4 million people), the Awakening was a trans-Atlantic Anglo-Saxon kind of movement.

In the Boston area, students at the Andover Theological Seminary in 1808 founded a secret society for missionary work. They called it the Brethren. In public they pushed for missions abroad, and in the course of the next sixty years they sent out something like two hundred missionaries. Out of this came the American Board of Commissioners for Foreign Missions, set up in 1810. Its missionaries came in large part from New England colleges like Williams, Amherst, and Dartmouth. Harvard, unfortunately, had already been lost to Unitarianism, but Yale was not. President Timothy Dwight of Yale, in his sermon before the American Board at Boston in 1813, foresaw a future in which "the Romish cathedral, the mosque, and the pagoda shall *not have one stone left upon another which shall not be thrown down.*" * He was really determined to move out and take care of the world.

Similarly, the American Board's eighteenth annual report in 1827 said that the object of foreign missions is "no less than the moral renovation of the world. Wars are to cease . . . Every village is to have its school and its church; every family its Bible, and the morning and evening prayer. The tabernacle of God is to be pitched among men." † Quite unlike the irresponsible American merchant abroad, making a profit however he could, the missionary was very full of a sense of responsibility for the spiritual fate of the heathen overseas. But he cast this responsibility in terms less of welfare than of Christian salvation through faith in Jesus Christ, exporting his own culture.

* Timothy Dwight, *A Sermon . . . before the American Board* (Boston, 1813), p. 26, cited in Clifton Jackson Phillips, *Protestant America and the Pagan World. The First Half Century of the American Board of Commissioners for Foreign Missions, 1810–1860* (Cambridge, Massachusetts: Harvard University Press, 1969), p. 1.

†Ibid., p. 12.

Since the early Protestant missionaries in the Anglo-American diaspora moved into the Far East by way of the Near East, naturally they followed the same pattern of activity they had developed at home in missions to the American Indians and then in the Near East. They believed in the efficacy of the Bible for anybody who could understand it. Therefore it was very important to begin translating the Good Word into the local languages. In the Mediterranean they set up a center at Malta for the translation of Scripture and the writing of tracts. In the Ottoman empire they did the same, and when they got to China, they continued in the same style. Professor Suzanne Barnett has catalogued in the Harvard-Yenching Library some one hundred twenty-nine early publications by missionaries in Chinese. These included many tracts, edifying stories, parables, and explanatory writings in Chinese, including magazines and geographies of the world. These publications reflected the effort by missionaries still excluded from the interior to reach their intended converts. The printed word, they found, had useful prestige in China.

Once they became established in the ports, they found that medical missionaries were also effective in establishing contact with the Chinese. Peter Parker of Yale is only the most famous of the early evangelist doctors who treated Chinese of all levels, including occasional officials. They also began schools for converts, as the British were doing.

After 1860, when missionaries had more chance of getting into the provinces, their work fell very soon into a general pattern. They had trouble in the cities. There they faced Confucian scholars, members of the Chinese ruling class, who would not stand for their presence, because what they were spreading was quite subversive of Confucianism. Missionaries at this time were not supporters of the established order. They were revolutionaries from the outside, for their teaching was essentially an attack on Confucianism and on the Confucian social order. This was potentially much more devastating than mere communism, a Western heresy, could ever be in America of the 1950's. The missionaries, for instance, were against ancestor reverence, against filial piety in any form. They were against idols of all sorts, even including kitchen gods, those rather harmless deities who sometimes may help a person out. They condemned grave offerings as idolatry, although presumably they were not against putting flowers on graves in their own country on Decoration Day. Their very different articles of faith determined whether Chinese actions were good or bad. When the Confucian filial son swept the grave of his ancestor and left an offering, that was bad in the early missionary view. Of course they were against obvious evils like child marriage, infanticide, and foot-binding, and also against opium, which the other foreigners were bringing in more and more.

Essentially, the early missionaries formed a Christian sect, insofar as they made converts, which they did only slowly. This sect had been declared heterodox as early as 1724, and so the missionaries tended to get away from the cities, where the ruling class didn't like them, and where the scholars, when they met for examinations in the Confucian classics, might even start riots and set a mob to tear down Christian buildings. Missionaries might be attacked, sometimes they were killed. In the countryside, on the other hand, they found farmers, and since most of the missionaries came from farm backgrounds, these Chinese were people they could understand —simple country folk who were polite, civilized Chinese, but illiterate. Steeped in superstition and folk religion, they saw Protestant Christianity as still another sect.

In the cities the Chinese literati regarded Christianity as outright superstition and were constantly getting after the missionaries. When told about the Virgin Birth, the literati asked, "How do you account for that? Could you do that again; if not, how do you know it happened? It's not common sense." They also pointed out that from a Confucian point of view, getting men and women together in a church or hall, although the women would sit on one side and the men on the other in those days, was very immoral. If the two sexes were gathered in the same room, all kinds of illicit ideas might arise in their imaginations, because they were only human. "We know what human beings are like. We have seen them in action. The idea that people of one sex should sit anywhere near people of the opposite sex is both anti-Confucian and immoral."

The Chinese attack on Christianity in the 1860's revived some of the themes and writings that had been used against the Jesuits in China in the seventeenth century. This included the usual Chinese punning. Catholic Christianity was called the religion of the Lord of Heaven (*t'ien-chu-chiao*—"the heaven's lord religion"). These sounds could also mean, with different characters, "the heavenly pig's grunt." Some Chinese zealots produced forthright pornographic writings attacking the missionaries for their immorality, and these they distributed widely.

Such activities created a severe problem for the Chinese government. As of 1867, here is the governor of Kiangsu reporting to the throne: "the converts rely on the missionaries. The missionaries rely on the foreign consuls. The foreign consuls hold the local officials responsible, and the local officials, if they are concerned with the general welfare, cannot but accommodate [the Christians]. Averting calamity in this fashion [the local officials thus] add fuel to the fire at the same time that they would extinguish it." * In other words, the missionaries and their converts were a continuing menace to the prestige of the Chinese government in the highest stratum of its own people.

The outcome of all this missionary effort by 1869 was that there were something like 400 missionaries on the scene, and not many more than 5,000 converts. In other words, not much success in numerical terms to reflect the first lifetime of effort.

What was the Chinese view of the Americans up to this point? How did the Chinese counter the American activity? At the outset they were confused about the American social order. The Americans seemed to be organized in tribes, since the states were known as *pu*, and *pu* is the term for a Mongol tribe. The USA had begun as thirteen tribes, and then had expanded into twenty tribes, or twenty-five tribes. They had a chieftain who was in Washington, which was named for the founder of USA.

The Chinese at first tried to borrow the foreign

* Li Han-chang, governor of Kiangsu and concurrently acting governor-general of Hunan and Hupei, quoted in Paul A. Cohen, *China and Christianity: The Missionary Movement and the Growth of Chinese Antiforeignism, 1860–1870* (Cambridge, Massachusetts: Harvard University Press, 1963), p. 163.

technology and get guns and ships of the Western type to repel the Western invaders. Chinese strategists also used the old idea of setting one Westerner against another—the British against the French, the French against the Americans, and so forth. But that was a knee-jerk reaction on the part of tradition-bound Chinese officials. Soon they moved on to a more sophisticated long-term strategy. After the first Opium War of 1840–1842 had been followed by the second war and eventually by the treaty settlement of 1860, Peking tried a program of appeasement—that is, to control the foreigners by trade. This was known in Chinese as *chi-mi,* "controlling with a loose rein." Even though the horse is stronger than you are, you are smarter than the horse, you hope. So you give him a loose rein, and then you can pull him in whenever necessary. This ancient concept was applied to the foreigner in this way: the foreigner is allowed to trade, and so the trade becomes a vested interest to him; if you then threaten to close down the trade, the foreigner comes to terms. This had been tried out with the East India Company many times at Canton and it had always worked. On that basis Peking felt that the new unequal trade treaties could be used to let the foreigner come and trade, but only so long as he respected the treaties.

Another traditional method the Chinese used in dealing with the foreigner in the nineteenth century was to put him in certain coastal areas where he had residential rights within limits. These turned out to be the treaty ports, but if the foreigner had been weak, they would have been ghettos. As it was, the ports were bases from which the Westerners could expand. China in the treaties also gave the foreigner the right to have his own local headman, as the Arabs had had their headmen to be the representatives of this whole national community. The Western headman turned out to be a consul who represented the foreign legal system and looked after the treaty rights of the foreign residents.

China had also followed the medieval custom of letting the Arabs, for instance, use their own law for their own people. How could you expect them to follow Chinese law when they could not read Chinese? This turned into extraterritoriality; and foreign consular jurisdiction became a system under which the foreigner had his own way more and more.

On these various grounds the Chinese accepted the treaty system in 1842 and 1843, and the Americans copied it from the British in 1844. By 1860, the Chinese knew that they could not split the barbarians apart. They had to accept the demands of the British and French at Peking in 1860, but they arranged that there would be no audience for foreign ministers with the emperor because he was a minor. In this way Peking could keep some of the tribute system functioning. They had always expected the kotow from the envoy of any foreign potentate. If he wanted to come to China, that was how he should behave. And the traditional tribute missions did indeed continue to come from the states around China after 1860—from Korea, Liu-ch'iu, Vietnam, and such places. In this situation the American minister John Ward came to China in 1859 to exchange ratifications of the 1858 treaty that the Americans had copied from the British when the British were fighting for it. Mr. Ward felt that he should follow his instructions to go to the capital and exchange ratifications, and so he accepted the Chinese terms and went in a cart, which is a tributary style of travel. Anybody who rode in a cart 90 miles from Tientsin to Peking over the roads of that day (a North China cart has no springs and is indestructible; it will destroy you before itself) had a real tributary experience. When Mr. Ward got to Peking, he refused to kotow (lie on the ground with his face on the floor), but he bowed and got his treaty ratification. (His remark, "I kneel only to God and to woman," if the Chinese understood it, must have seemed very quaint.) The British felt that he had lowered the flag in a most unseemly manner.

The egalitarian Americans were much the least grand of all the foreign powers. The Russians, the British, and the French all had a good deal more considered policy behind their activities. Through the treaty settlement they were all taken into the Chinese power structure —that is, they were given a capacity to operate in China, semigovernmentally, among their own people, to participate in the control of certain major centers that were treaty ports, and to use their shipping on Chinese waters. All these and other privileges were infringements of Chinese sovereignty, or you might say they were a sharing of Chinese sovereignty with the foreigners, including the Americans. Of all the powers, the Americans had been the least aggressive.

In analyzing the treaty system, we must distinguish between the Ch'ing dynasty, which made the treaty arrangements, and the Chinese population. The Chinese people as a whole were submerged below the political level and not active in affairs of state. They were not yet nationalistic. They were pre-modern and did not have much say in what went on. The Ch'ing dynasty accepted the Westerners into the Chinese state structure in order to survive. The Westerners were powerful barbarians, but the dynasty could get their help against the rebels who so heavily beset it in this period. In retrospect the Ch'ing suppression of the Taiping rebels between 1850 and 1864 with the help of Western arms to keep itself in power looks like domestic feudalism using foreign imperialism. In the Marxist terminology of today, the Americans were imperialists.

Yet to the American side of this early relationship, China up to this point presented a very different aspect. Whereas China was seen as a field of adventure and enterprise for private individuals, it was not an object of great national concern at the governmental level. The United States sent a commissioner out to China occasionally, but didn't bother to send a paid consul until 1854, and thereafter had no thought of sending specially trained consular officers. Merchant consuls were appointed for the most part. Up to 1870 Americans developed no lasting substantial China trade interests. No big firms remained active after the failure of Russell and Company in 1877. There was no lobby that could operate in this country. The China trade had risen and subsided.

Similarly, there was as yet no missionary lobby. To be sure, the Chinese were steeped in backwardness and heathenism; they were remnants of an ancient civilization in decay. They should be the recipients of our benevolence and paternalism. But the mission movement was not yet organized in the businesslike fashion it was soon to assume.

All this was summed up, I think, in the Burlingame mission. Anson Burlingame had been the American minister in Peking in the 1860's in a period of general

cooperation after the treaty settlement. When he retired
from this post, the Chinese made him head of a delegation
to negotiate treaties with the Western powers, and as he
came through the United States in 1868 he began to make
speeches about "planting the shining cross on every hill
and in every valley" of China, the opening of a great new
day. He summed up some of the American shrewdness,
sentiment, and benevolent concern that we have seen in
the record. When he appeared in Boston, the occasion was
celebrated by Oliver Wendell Holmes. He wrote a very
fine poem which says something about the American view
of China even today. There are passages that we may be
able to quote with benefit tomorrow or the next day. It
begins:

Brothers, whom we may not reach
Through the veil of alien speech,
Welcome! welcome! eyes can tell
What the lips in vain would spell, —
Words that hearts can understand,
Brothers from the Flowery Land!

We, the evening's latest born,
Hail the children of the morn!
We, the new creation's birth,
Greet the lords of ancient earth,
From their storied walls and towers
Wandering to these tents of ours!

Land of wonders, fair Cathay,
Who long hast shunned the staring day,
Hid in mists of poet's dreams
By the blue and yellow streams, —
Let us thy shadowed form behold, —
Teach us as thou didst of old.

Knowledge dwells with length of days;
Wisdom walks in ancient ways:
Thine the compass that could guide
A nation o'er the stormy tide,
Scourged by passions, doubts, and fears,
Safe through thrice a thousand years!

Looking from thy turrets gray
Thou hast seen the world's decay, —
Egypt drowning in her sands, —
Athens rent by robbers' hands, —
Rome, the wild barbarian's prey,
Like a storm-cloud swept away:

Looking from thy turrets gray
Still we see thee. Where are they?
And lo! a new-born nation waits,
Sitting at the golden gates
That glitter by the sunset sea, —
Waits with outspread arms for thee!

Open wide, ye gates of gold,
To the Dragon's banner-fold!
Builders of the mighty wall,
Bid your mountain barriers fall!
So may the girdle of the sun
Bind the East and West in one,

Till Mount Shasta's breezes fan
The Snowy peaks of Ta Sieue-Shan, —
Till Erie blends its waters blue
With the waves of Tung-Ting-Hu, —
Till deep Missouri lends its flow
To swell the rushing Hoang-Ho!

Oliver Wendell Holmes,
Complete Poetical Works

II

CHRISTIAN EDUCATION:
A SUCCESS STORY—
THE 1870's TO THE 1930's

Missionary work in education in China is a subject that requires careful periodization if it is to be understood historically. The missionary's role in China's process of change varied fundamentally between one era and another. Although the successive generations of missionaries themselves changed profoundly in their aims and ideas, their function in the Chinese scene changed even more. From outlandish subversives and enemies of the old order, they were transformed into pillars of a new, though temporary, establishment.

Missionaries going to China, of course, wanted converts, but they had to settle for what they could get. They branched out into a good many other activities, particularly education. The Christian education that they offered in China met a need at a certain time and in certain circumstances, in an era of disorder during a dynastic interregnum and a period of incipient revolution. In this transition period, missionary educators contributed to China's modernization and set certain styles for the new

China. But they lost out as soon as the revolution came, for it expressed the national aspirations of a newly patriotic people. This sequence of acceptance and rejection has colored our relations with China.

First, in the era of beginnings, look at the setting in which the Christian missionary colleges got started in the nineteenth century, and then look at their era of opportunity in the first part of the twentieth century when they performed important services to the Chinese people during a period of revolutionary change. One of these services consisted in educating a part of the urban middle class, children of what is now called the bourgeois élite. Thereby, the Christian colleges quite easily became targets of the new nationalist movement because they were foreign-run institutions. On the other hand, they became targets of the communist movement because they were middle class.

In this connection, one may ask whether the Chinese Communists have not been distributing to the Chinese people a number of things in which the missionaries themselves had pioneered. Perhaps these Americans can legitimately creep in the door of the Chinese revolution and claim to have made a certain contribution to it, even though the Chinese public on the mainland today does not recognize the fact.

In the course of time no doubt we can expect Chinese opinion to come around from the extreme revolutionary view of today to a more even-handed attitude as history moves farther back, just as we in our own thinking have to reduce the high estimates we like to make of all American contributions abroad.

The Christian educators in China have to be understood as a small but eventually influential minority in a rather small social scene. In the nineteenth century the Chinese ruling class and government bureaucracy, the whole leadership element, was remarkably small considering the size of the country. It took something like 40,000 officials at most to run this empire of 400 million people. Bureaucracy had been well developed over the centuries but had not yet proliferated in the modern manner. Consequently, even the small number of missionaries and the small numbers of institutions and students involved in the Christian educational efforts could be of considerable importance, because China at the literate, upper level was still a rather small society. In contrast, the Chinese Communist regime has been dispensing a new model of life to the whole mass of the people.

Another factor in the American missionaries' work in China was China's slow rate of economic and social growth compared with the more advanced countries. China did grow in this period, from the middle of the nineteenth century to the middle of the twentieth, but it fell behind the industrialized sector of the world. This can be illustrated by the various aspects of the American involvement in China. The American firms in 1870 totaled about 50; and by 1930, 550. The number of missionaries in 1870 was about 200 or so, representing twelve societies from the United States; by 1930 it was about 3,000, representing perhaps 45 societies. Between 1900 and 1930, the six early missionary colleges grew to sixteen, counting Catholic as well as Protestant institutions. The 130 schools of 1900 grew to 200 in 1930; in the same period 70 hospitals doubled to 150. The number of Chinese students coming to the United States annually in 1919 was under 1,000; by 1930 it was about 1,400. American trade with China increased about fifteen times between the 1870's and the 1930's, and even then, it amounted to only 3 or 4 percent of America's total world trade. The framework of growth and change in which the missionaries were working in China was rather modest by world standards.

The underdevelopment was evident particularly in trade. Americans sold some cotton textiles to the Chinese but found that kerosene and cigarettes were the things that sold in greatest quantities. Kerosene is the simplest of commodities, certainly not a highly manufactured product of Western industry. Cigarettes, also, are rather easily produced. There wasn't enough purchasing power in China for more complicated things, and the China trade did not grow beyond an elementary level. China did not become a colonial economy of the kind that used to supply a metropolitan colonial power with vast amounts of raw materials, these materials being sold back to the colonial dependent after conversion into manufactured goods. In China no plantation production for export developed.

Let us set the missionary in this context in the late nineteenth century, remembering that he came primarily to save souls. Some scholars have taken the letters of application to mission boards to try to get a generalized picture of the applicant for missionary work. Who is he? or, Who is she? (A bisexual pronoun would be useful here.) He usually is a farm boy, or a small town boy, not a city boy. He usually has experienced a self-conversion, he has received a call, maybe after a revival meeting, and has come to the conclusion that he should offer himself for service abroad.

Typically, a recruit got theological training for two years, perhaps more. It was a sort of higher education for its day and place. The young missionary usually became highly literate, and probably studied a foreign language in the process. Before he left for his mission work, he was likely to find a mate and get married. A woman wanting to go abroad as a missionary could indeed go as a single woman (about a third of the missionary body consisted of single women), but the majority going overseas were couples, self-contained units, as they hoped to be.

The missionary couple, after their sea voyage, which was still a fairly lengthy and sometimes arduous experience, now arrive in China. They are immediately struck by the condition of the common people. They find that for transport they can ride in a cart or on a barrow or in a sedan chair, or, after 1870, they can ride in a ricksha. The ricksha combines ball bearings and wire wheels of the bicycle type with a human horse. The first time the foreigner rides behind a human horse, he may feel it is degrading to the human horse. Yet very soon, when he has to go somewhere in a hurry, or when he is feeling tired, he is glad to climb into a ricksha. The foreigner adapts himself to the custom of the country pretty rapidly. No doubt there were missionaries who said, "No, I shall never ride behind somebody pulling me, I shall always walk," but few such statements are recorded. It was not feasible to live by that non-Chinese ideal in nineteenth- and early twentieth-century China. The argument always came up, "If the ricksha man can't get a fare, how does he live?" Thus the foreigner learned very quickly that China had an overabundance of people. Their muscles must be used for motive power in place of machines.

The missionary also found dirt and disease, poverty and ignorance, all of which wear the people down. But the missionary might well feel that the worst thing was the heathenism. In his subjective attitude he might feel that dirt, poverty, disease, and ignorance could be alleviated if the word of God were properly accepted. Perhaps this was a non sequitur, but I doubt that it seemed so in his mind. He was devoted to the idea of preaching in order to bring people to the religious experience that he had had, to join him in a consecration to high ideals.

The youthfulness of most missionaries on their arrival abroad undoubtedly colored their whole enterprise. Normally they were young people in their twenties, not yet established in the world, full of idealistic determination and necessarily insecure except in their sense of faith. Meeting the alien culture of China gave them an on-the-job training for which they were not prepared by maturity of experience elsewhere. They were fresh and often untried products of their native culture.

Since the young missionary wanted to start preaching as soon as he could, he began serious language study immediately. The Chinese language was essential to reach the people. Thus, along with the diplomatic interpreters, missionaries become thorough language students. This led them into the business of writing tracts, as one way to reach the common man, if he was literate. They also got started itinerating among out stations in villages, and this they found pleasant because it got them out into the countryside among a less critical audience.

The mission stations that harbored these evangelists tended to be rather self-concerned and somewhat ingrown establishments. Studies of mission stations indicate that the principals spent a great deal of their time thinking about their internal problems of organization and personal status. They faced the problem of raising the funding from back home—perhaps the home constituency could be persuaded to provide $100 more each year. They also had problems of doctrinal difference. Brother Jonathan might want to teach in English, but this might strike Brother William as preparing the students for an urban commercial life that would be quite lost to Jesus. Arguing over this, they can seek guidance in prayer, but if their prayers lead them in different directions, they may never agree. All kinds of personal squabbles arose in a mission station, just as in any beleaguered or confined group.

The small Christian community in a station —consisting of two or three couples with perhaps an un-married female missionary—was likely to find that the first converts came from among the servants or the teachers—the people who were being paid. Converts were not easily made in nineteenth-century China. In mid-century, the pioneer missionary might not make any converts for the first five or even ten years of his service. Yet he stayed in the field, working hard every day, praying morning and night, leading a religious life and trying to lead others to his religion.

This experience naturally set up a great challenge to the missionary's sense of adequacy. On his local front in China he often suffered frustration, but on his home front in America he had to maintain a proper appearance of determination and progress. He therefore sent back his accounts of how he was doing this, this, and this, and sometimes with a good deal of quantification—he had preached so many sermons, itinerated to so many places, talked to so many people. On the strength of this recorded effort he hoped that the church at home would give him further support. He persevered in the face of adversity, taking it as a test of character. This accorded with the fact that he had been inspired to evangelism from a rural or small-town parochial background, where "everybody" agreed on what was right and worthy. He had a message of the utmost importance to convey to other people, a message that related to their salvation and their future in the afterlife.

Sustained by his convictions though often frustrated in the action of saving souls, the China missionary as a dedicated man of good will was likely to find his life preempted by the immediate practical problems of the larger Chinese community. The Chinese people needed help, and this became the reason for his being among them.

This partly explains why missionaries went into education, although evangelism remained their primary aim. Some years ago a group of retired missionaries, among them Dr. Kenneth Scott Latourette, the great scholar of missions worldwide, had a discussion about what had happened to the Christian effort in China. This was about 1950, after it had been pretty well eclipsed by the revolution. The group kept coming back to the thought that perhaps the missionaries had gone astray in embarking on educational and social service good works. They should have stayed with evangelism and the building of Christian character. This was an issue much debated by missionaries in the nineteenth century. They themselves had had to study Chinese in order to bring the Good Book to the Chinese people, and also to educate a Chinese pastorate. Education came on their agenda because a Chinese pastor, like the missionary, had to be educated by instruction in a theological school or something equivalent. Schools for the young Chinese were started not only in the interests of literacy but in the hope that out of a small group of boys would come some who could become Chinese Christian pastors to carry on the good work.

The early schools provided a means of contact between evangelists and Chinese. To the children of converts they offered something of value. Education for the common man in China was considered a great opportunity, and many children who came to missionary schools were frankly sent in order to learn to read and write. Since they were not upper-class children, education was their chief hope of rising in the world.

Similarly, medical missions proved useful as a way for the missionaries to reach the public and find converts. Soon the three great missionary institutions were the street chapel for preaching, the school, and the dispensary, the last often eventually turning into a hospital. Of the three, however, missionary educational activity became the most innovative and influential. Christian proselytism produced by 1906 some 178,000 Protestant converts. (Figures differ, but there were less than 200,000 in the early twentieth century.) Later in the century the Chinese Christian community totaled a third of a million, but never rose above half a million. It was hardly 1 percent of the population. If the missionary enterprise was a failure in terms of numbers of converts, on the educational side, a great deal was achieved. The missionary interacted with his Chinese environment and in many cases had a profound influence on it.

First of all, having set up a school to teach the

Chinese to read and write their own language, the missionary educator faced the question of whether he should add English and science. If he added science to his curriculum, as did some pioneers, like Calvin Mateer in Shantung, he found very soon that English was also needed, because you can't go very far in modern science just translating and inventing new Chinese terms on a local basis. Western science manuals were required, so textbooks of science were soon produced in Chinese; however, English also was taught. World history and world geography were also brought in. Eventually some of the bright products of these early schools were sent abroad in missionary channels to be educated in the West. Rather quickly the returned student became an element in Chinese life. Thus education, once begun, leads on of its own inner momentum, and its expansion cannot be stopped.

In all this process of building a new Chinese Christian community, the missionary provided social leadership for a different style of life and different values. I suppose you might say they were "modern." He aimed first of all at the common man in China, not at the ruling class, which generally had repulsed him. He was for the individual as against the demands of family. He was for women's emancipation. He was for the application of scientific technology. Inevitably, the stimulus of Western example led the Chinese into bigger ideas of nationalism and reform.

Out of this early period in the nineteenth century, there emerged Chinese reformers who had had contact with missionaries. In many cases they had become converts in the sense that they accepted baptism or something similar even though they did not become known in Chinese history as Christians. Such men were certainly influenced by the Christian tradition and at the time often were regarded by missionaries as converts. Whether one is a Christian is a little bit like whether one is a Communist. It is a matter of opinion. The card-carrying Communist party member that we used to hunt for back in the 1950's is hard to define in precise terms, unless he carries his card with him all the time. When one looks back at the equally subversive activity of Christians in China a century ago, it is hard to say if a Chinese was strictly or thoroughly a Christian convert, unless he became a Christian pastor. There were, in short, many people in the annals of modern China who stood forth as reformers, and who were at the time regarded by missionaries as Christians.

Professor Paul Cohen has studied a number of these "Christian reformers." They include such people as Yung Wing, the first Chinese graduate of Yale, who came back to the United States in 1872 as head of a mission to train a hundred or so Chinese students in towns in the Connecticut valley. Many of these students later reached high positions in China. Other Christian-influenced reformers were pioneer journalists and early advocates of the recovery of Chinese rights from the West by the reform of the treaty system. Some, like T'ang Shao-yi or Wu T'ing-fang, studied enough law in the West and knew enough English in a bicultural way to argue China's case in legal terms and demand restoration of Chinese rights. There were other eminent professed Christians, for example, Sun Yat-sen, who lived part of his life in Hawaii as a child, got his education in Hong Kong, and spoke English as well as Chinese. He had a Western background, as well as a Chinese background. Bilingual missionaries produced bicultural converts.

Missionary work in education led on to good works of a broader range. Some missionaries became journalists, like one man from Georgia, Young J. Allen, who published a Chinese journal, *News of the Churches (Chiao-hui hsin-pao)* beginning in 1868, and eventually turned it into an international magazine, *The Globe Magazine (Wan-kuo kung-pao)* or *News of the World*. He spread reform ideas that were eagerly picked up by Chinese scholars. The missionaries in the late nineteenth century, in effect, provided the textual wherewithal for the reform of Chinese institutions. And so the Reform Movement of the 1890's received a considerable input from missionary sources. After Japan's defeat of China in 1895, famous reformers such as Timothy Richard, a Welsh Baptist, and Gilbert Reid, an American Presbyterian, even got to the point of setting up a special missionary effort to reach the Chinese official class. They could do this at the end of the century when the Chinese were in trouble with many imperialist powers. These particular missionaries had their day in Peking in 1896, 1897, and 1898. They were able to see high officials very extensively. They urged reforms of all kinds, including Christianity.

It was in this atmosphere of rising receptivity and increased opportunity after 1895 that the Christian colleges got started. Of course there was a common bond between Americans and Chinese in their belief in education as a chief means of human advancement. For the American and Chinese common man, there was also a common interest in egalitarianism. It is an interesting and striking fact that the Christian colleges were nearly all American, not British—the British joined in one or two of them, participating in the creation of colleges only by joining other groups. Otherwise, all the sixteen Christian colleges in China were essentially American or American and Canadian. Why was this? I suggest that it reflects the respective social backgrounds of the British and American missionaries. The American Protestants came from denominational colleges, first in New England, then in the Middle West. They were part of the spread of education through denominational colleges that took place in the United States. Colleges like Oberlin, Grinnell, and Carlton were created by men who came from Amherst, Williams, and Dartmouth. Missionaries to China naturally began to spread this sort of college; it was part of their home culture. Indeed, the American liberal arts college that grew out of these denominational colleges took root in many countries through missionary channels. Witness Robert College in Istanbul, the American University in Beirut, and others in India, Korea, Japan, the Philippines, and elsewhere.

In contrast, the British Protestants came from a different, more stratified society and from its lower class. For the most part they did not have a university background. British missionaries had had grammar school education but not college education. So they did not establish colleges.

Another factor in the growth of the Christian colleges was that by the time the American colleges were getting started in China another wave of missionary activity and organization had been initiated in the United States. This second phase of growth in the missionary movement was marked in the 1870's and 1880's by the reorganization of mission boards to get the missionary movement on a more businesslike basis. Boards began to be headed by laymen administrators, executives who could raise money and manage these early transnational agencies. They were sending out people to maintain stations or agencies abroad. They had to recruit the people for the purpose, train them, finance them, and handle their travel and communications. This was a big executive operation. Most important, the mission boards in this period developed more substantial sources of funding, and these later provided some support for Christian colleges. In this same period the YMCA spread to China. Begun in England in the 1840's, it was by the 1880's bringing young men in Chinese urban centers into a Christian environment and giving them help in adjusting to city life.

Curiously, this same era saw an anti-Chinese labor movement in the United States, east as well as west, but particularly in California. Not only was American labor fearful of the competition of Chinese immigrants. There was also a fear of their propagating "Oriental" diseases (the germ theory was becoming popular as the latest medical wisdom) and a dislike of their strange ways and apparent unassimilability. The first Oriental exclusion acts were passed at the same time that interest in missions was reawakening. Evidently they were not mutually exclusive concerns.

The new missionary interest of the 1880's was expressed in the American colleges in the Student Volunteer Movement for Foreign Missions. Typically it was active in the denominational colleges of the Middle West.

It recruited young student missionaries and, beginning in the latter part of the nineteenth century, sent several thousand volunteers abroad in mission work, the largest single area being China. With this movement came activity on college campuses to support missions abroad, and a vogue of college graduates going into missionary careers. They were backed at the end of the century by a layman's movement which could maintain their financing. From these sources derived the American leadership in the Christian colleges in China.

By the end of the century there were a number of these institutions that had gradually been built up from schools: two in Shantung that eventually merged, three in Peking or just outside, several around Shanghai. They had a total of about 164 students in 1900—not many—just a bare beginning. But major mission stations with schools had got to the point of inaugurating a college department, staffing it at first with missionaries and their wives.

The time of great opportunity for American missionaries began in the period after the Boxer Rebellion of 1900. During four decades, in the midst of war and revolution, they had a chance to provide an educational service that was to have many ramifications and repercussions. In the first place, the antiforeignism that reached high tide in the Boxer movement had been discredited. It was plain that China must accept foreign contact for some time to come, still on the foreigner's terms. Moreover, the classics were now questioned. Confucianism was on the way out. The examination system in the Confucian classics ended in 1905. The government became comparatively weaker at the center, whereas foreign influence became greater all over China.

By 1905 there were six Christian colleges, and by 1925, thirteen (sixteen, counting the three Catholic institutions). They were mainly supplied with students from some 330 Protestant middle schools, which enrolled 25,000 students and thus provided a pool of talent for the Christian colleges. Graduates of these high schools or middle schools set up by mission stations all over the country—and 330 is a lot of middle schools—already had a start in English, which by this time was essential for the education offered by the colleges.

This flowering of colleges was part of a much broader trend: the missionary movement's creation of a variety of new institutions to meet the problems of Chinese life. For example, hospitals grew up in the same way. In 1876 there had been 16 hospitals; in 1925 there were 300, half of them American. Medical schools were then set up, again under missionary auspices. Mission boards branched out into still other good works. Nanking University, one of the missionary colleges, set up a school of agriculture and forestry. Soon it got into farm extension work, Cornell style; and pioneers like J. Lossing Buck sent their students out into the villages to find out how the farmers did things, and whether they could be helped with modern agronomic science. The China International Famine Relief Commission also was organized with missionaries pushing it. By 1936 the Famine Relief Commission had collected something like $50 million for spending in China. They dug 5,000 wells and built 2,000 miles of roads, and a lot of canals. They moved in with these public works in the warlord period, at a time when Chinese government was so broken up that nothing much was being done in the public interest. The foreigner came

in and did it. Beginning in the late 1920's, the rural reconstruction movement tried to reach the village, organize
the people to achieve literacy, and bring in various kinds
of technology to raise living standards.

This is how missionaries and other foreigners in
China moved in to fill a vacuum. After all, if a Chinese
leadership had been doing these things at all adequately,
there would not have been so much opportunity for the
missionary. He would have been nosing in. As it was,
however, he was on the spot, saw the problems and the
solutions that could be offered, and took action. This is a
feature of the pre-Liberation period, before 1949, of
which the public in China today is quite unaware. I don't
know who is going to tell them about it. No doubt the first
thing to note and remember is that no missionary or other
foreigner in China ever did anything without Chinese
help. Today's patriots may be assured that these new
developments were in large part Chinese, even when
foreign-led or financed.

In this context of Chinese need and foreign opportunity, let us look very briefly at how the colleges were set
up. There were difficult problems to be overcome. Indi-
vidualistic missionaries who functioned as representatives of established constituencies were not easily assimi-
lated in new institutions. It was a long process with a lot of
squabbling back and forth, a lot of negotiating. Remember
that the missionaries were not only all individualists; they
were also extremely fragmented through sect differentia-
tions. Take the Methodists in China. There were four
kinds: Canadian Methodists, English Methodists, American Methodists South (from the Civil War era), and
American Methodists North. The Methodists alone, in

other words, were four different groups and did not operate as a unit at all. The Baptists and Presbyterians were equally broken up.

As Jessie Lutz points out in her basic volume on the China colleges, uniting schools to make colleges became easier after 1900 because the missionaries had got acquainted in the disasters of that year, when many leaders had been in the Peking legations. Also, many had lost their property, and some institutions had been burned down and had to be rebuilt. They might as well make a coordinated effort. When they got compensation, it was to their advantage to pool their resources. Soon they found themselves in competition with the government schools that were being set up in the Manchu dynasty's reform movement after 1902, and this spurred their united action.

Out of this gradual process of conglomeration, the famous mission colleges acquired the names by which we know them in retrospect. In Shantung, for instance, colleges in three different places were finally put together; they represented twelve different mission societies. The result was called Cheloo University in 1915. In Nanking there were four different institutions that finally worked out a union, and Nanking University got that name in 1910. In Peking there were half a dozen institutions, one outside the city at Tungchow, and they negotiated for years to figure out how they could combine and still represent the mission board and the tradition that each one had behind it. They finally produced Yenching University, the most famous of the whole group, which, however, took that name only in 1928. The picture in Chengtu was very similar. There, there were Canadian and British boards operating; five different societies got together and

formed West China Union University in 1910. Meanwhile
Canton had the most trouble because there was so much
antiforeignism there. Lingnan at Canton emerged as a
nondenominational college, for which it was difficult to
get support. Of the three women's colleges, Chinling
College for Women at Nanking was the best known and
set a new standard in its particular line.

It is noteworthy that about half the Christian colleges are in the Shanghai area: in Nanking, Soochow,
Hangchow, or Shanghai, the area of the Yangtze delta.
This had been for centuries the economic center of the
country, a power center from which leadership came.

How did missionary education affect the Chinese
scene? What did it contribute? This is hard to evaluate.
The students at first were from the poor and the commoner class. But by degrees, as Western things gained
prestige and reform came into vogue, it became obvious
one must learn things from abroad and even from foreigners. As the great port cities grew up, more students came
to the Christian colleges from urban centers. Particularly
in Shanghai, of course, St. John's University had a real
middle-class student body.

At the same time, the old battle about whether to
teach English to students in a Christian college was finally settled. English is required, and the students who
know it best are likely to be from Christian middle
schools. In this way the foreign education has been a
self-perpetuating thing. It demands less Chinese classical
study of the student.

However, most of the students who go to a Christian college do not graduate. They attend, they get something, they develop their English, and then move on. The

graduates are mainly Christians, and they often get jobs in Christian institutions, where they continue in Christian work. It is a great problem to trace graduates of these institutions, since the record kept in the United States, the only one available, is in English. If you have long lists of names of graduates, for instance from Fukien Christian University, in the spelling of the Min dialect, you don't know for sure what the names are in Mandarin. It is a question whether we can ever find out who were the students in the Christian colleges.

However, we do know that the Christian colleges brought into China an American type of extracurricular activity—church services to begin with, and revival meetings, even itinerating in the countryside. All these, you may say, are methods to reach masses of people with a moral message. Thus a Christian college student, if he chooses to go to these revival meetings or itinerating in the countryside, has a kind of experience that Chinese scholars of the past have not usually had. A Christian college also is strong in physical education. There are many sports and much exercise, even military drill, the development of physique. There are also many social events. This kind of college is a very busy place. In fine, the academic community in these Christian colleges was quite different from the old-style Chinese community, and rather different in style from the order set in the new government-run universities of this period.

The Christian colleges also developed new professions, setting up nursing schools, library schools, schools of journalism, schools of law. The missionaries broke new ground in these professions, making new kinds of training available to small numbers of Chinese.

Against this background one can see where the missionaries eventually lost out, being like all of us culture-bound. They aimed to create Christian individuals, not to remake Chinese society. They had a profound influence, and helped start the revolution, but it wasn't their aim to do so. They were only trying to nurture new Christian personalities. This was because they had come from a pluralistic society which had a hard-won separation of church and state. The church was not supposed to reform the state. Missionary educators consequently had no political methods or ideas in mind. For that reason, they could not in the end fit into the Chinese revolutionary scene.

After the Boxer year, the China missionaries generally were anti-rebel. They felt they should let no political views come into Christian work. Here is the statement of the Centenary Conference in 1907, after a century of Protestant missions in China. They say to the faithful, "Be vigilant, lest in the present national awakening the Christian church should in any way be made use of for revolutionary ends, and lest Chinese Christians should through ignorance and confusion of thought or misdirected zeal be led into acts of disobedience against the government." This is of course very proper, apolitical. In 1910, here is another statement of the Edinburgh Conference: "Missionaries should keep clear of all party and faction. Missionaries should have nothing to do with political agitation. This is outside their sphere. Engaging in it can only harm their work." * The relation of the convert to the missionary is to be purely religious. This is sound

* Quoted in Leonard M. Outerbridge, *The Lost Churches of China* (Philadelphia: Westminster Press, 1952), p. 117.

sense for a foreigner in China. You should not get into local politics. But the result is, of course, that you miss the revolution. The missionary, even though he has helped to start it, cannot lead the revolution. Worse than this, he comes into conflict with Chinese nationalism.

This is the end of the story: a Chinese-American conflict of sentiments and interests. Of the many examples, one in particular, bearing on Yenching University, has been studied by Philip West. The leadership of this university in the 1920's and 1930's rested in an unusual group of Chinese Christian and American missionary educators. They had early formed a religious group called The Life Fellowship, through which they came to know each other intimately. As a group with common aims and a common concern about Christian ideals, they worked together the more easily in setting up the university and handling its affairs. Yenching, as the primary Christian college, benefited from the collaboration of this very able group of Chinese and Americans. But as early as 1922 an anti-Christian movement began in China's educational institutions. Although it came in with the ideas of the Soviet revolution along with Marxism-Leninism and the Communist party, the basic logic of the movement was nationalistic. It claimed that the Christian colleges were foreign institutions, a kind of imposition, controlled from abroad, which of course was true in form, pushing foreign ways, and buying people in. This political issue continued to bubble along in the 1920's, while the Nationalist revolution ran its course. Yenching saw some splitting up of its leadership, but carried on its work and accepted the Nationalist government requirement after 1928 that it register with the ministry of education and drop compulsory Christian worship.

The real crisis hit the Chinese Christian who was at once a patriot and a believer in an allegedly "foreign" faith. Some were very much torn by the fact that their basic object as patriots was not to bring China to Christ, but rather to bring China to survival and modernization. Some eventually went with the Nationalist movement and dropped their Christianity. Most did not, but from the 1920's on, the issue was joined.

The dénouement was postponed for twenty or thirty years by the Japanese attack on China, which began in 1915 in the 21 Demands, then in 1931 in full force in Manchuria, and in 1937 with all-out war. This was a body blow to China's modernization in general. The missionaries in the last decade or more of the Japanese attack became valuable colleagues of Chinese patriots, because the missionaries had their extraterritorial protection against Japan until 1941. They could stand out against the Japanese, communicate with the outside, get supplies in, and give protection in case of need. Thus thanks to Japan, Christian missionaries still had a role to play in a time of war for the survival of the Chinese state. Christianity had been undermined by that time, but it was not superseded by Marxism-Leninism and the Communist revolution until the late 1940's.

What, finally, was the contribution of missionary education to the Chinese revolution? It was a vehicle for Western influence; and its institutional contributions, I think, are quite numerous. In many lines it was a pilot model, and the revolution that came later picked up and used many of its achievements, sometimes consciously, sometimes unconsciously. First of all there was the idea of changing the individual—conversion. The Chinese Communists call it *fan-shen*, turning over. Then there was the idea of reaching the common man for this purpose, and that of course goes on today under Chairman Mao. Again, there was the missionary's opposition to the Confucian élite and its ruling class doctrine, his contrary espousal of literacy for all, together with missionary education that represented an intellectual emancipation in science, mathematics, and technology—all a new development of modern times. Added to this was missionary education for women and their general emancipation. The idea of sending Chinese abroad for training, the inauguration at home of famine relief, hospital care, and medical schools, all these things must be mentioned. The student study group, or *hsueh-hui*, a reformist group that got started at the end of the nineteenth century, undoubtedly had some missionary and YMCA background and influence behind it. Farm extension work, rural reconstruction, these too were parts of the missionary's extended contribution. It all remains to be appraised, and of course one of the problems is that the missionaries were not exclusively responsible for every innovation. Many Chinese were picking up useful new things from elsewhere.

In conclusion, I think we can say that like all foreigners in China, the missionaries by the 1940's had become part of China's ruling class—in our current parlance, part of the establishment. By the time the Communists came to power, there was no question that the missionaries were in a conservative position. They could not themselves lead the revolution. From their American background they could not supply either the ideas or the methods for a modern party-dictatorship, mass-mobilization, political revolution, and so they could easily be tagged as part of the establishment that had to be overthrown. And so they were.

III

POWER POLITICS: CONCEPTS AND MISCONCEPTIONS, 1898 TO 1972

In the first chapter, on the beginnings of American merchant and missionary activity in China down to 1870, there is one point that I hope sticks in memory. That is that Americans came to China as country cousins of the British, under the wing of the British empire. In the second chapter, on Christian education, I pointed out that its status was based on the right of extraterritoriality, which the British had originally secured. Christian colleges were incorporated in the United States, but able to function in China. They had their big opportunity during an interlude when the Chinese government was weak. Even when it became stronger, the attack by Japan made the Western establishment in China still acceptable to the Chinese.

Out of this early experience before 1941, I think a certain sentiment about China accumulated among the American public, a somewhat possessive sentiment. China became our favorite charity, so to speak. But at the same time the Americans accumulated rather little experience of responsibility in China on the part of the United States government. This is the theme pursued in this third chapter, under four headings: the most-favored nation approach, the me-too tradition; the Open Door and what that was seen to stand for; the American private participation in Chinese life; and finally the American government policy regarding China since 1941.

First, as to our most-favored nation approach to China. Translated from international law into common parlance, most-favored nation means "me-too." The unequal treaties with China all had this provision in effect, "If you hereafter give any further privileges to anyone else, then we get them too." On this basis, China became a land of adventure and opportunity, an interesting experience for many private Americans. The American government supported them from time to time, when necessary, but not as a great effort of policy. It was not necessary. The treaty system that conferred the privileges was maintained by others.

In this way the American policy tradition toward China grew up out of a number of bits and pieces that affected government activity, but without any realistic formulation of the fact that our basic policy position, had been given us by the warfare of others and was not even sustained by our own efforts.

One tradition was that of the naval diplomat who went to China and requested certain privileges or opportunities for trade. Commodore Kearny, Commodore Biddle, Commodore Perry (in Japan), Admiral Rodgers, Commodore Shufeldt in Korea—these naval officers all made forward moves in American policy. There was also a tradition of sending commissioners from Washington (our term until 1860 for diplomatic ministers). Men like Caleb Cushing, Humphrey Marshall, Robert McLane, William B. Reed, and John E. Ward represented the United States in certain periods on a rather *ad hoc* basis. They were political figures drawn from public life, with no background concerning China until they got there.

Out of this grew up a tradition of reliance on China hands, men on the spot who could be asked to handle things whenever a naval diplomat or a politician-commissioner was not available. These old hands were missionary diplomats. Peter Parker, the missionary eye doctor from Yale, was the American secretary of legation, and then for a time the American commissioner. Samuel Wells Williams, who came to Yale afterward, was secretary of legation for a long time and acting minister in certain periods. Parallel to this use of missionaries there was also a long tradition of using American merchants as merchant consuls, particularly the partners of Russell and Company—men named Forbes, Delano, Cunningham.

From this use of China hands to represent American interests there developed a tradition of cooperation with the established order of the treaty system. The cooperative policy of the 1860's pursued by Minister Anson Burlingame was echoed in the 1890's by Minister Charles Denby, who stayed in Peking so long that he became head of the diplomatic corps.

I think we can only conclude that the United States government down to 1898 had a non-power policy in China. It was not engaging in power politics there. It was present only on a me-too basis. It did not face the hard choices, and they sometimes were quite hard to make when it came to the use of force, whereas the British faced and did make these choices, as did even the French at certain times. The American policy was not to use force, but merely to get what anybody else got, to wait until another power acted, and then pick up whatever was available by invoking the most-favored nation clause.

Here is an instruction from Secretary of State Lewis Cass in 1857 to William B. Reed, the commissioner in China. There was a war going on. The British and the French expeditionary forces were trying to cement the treaty system and get the unequal treaty privileges finally accepted by Peking. The Secretary of State said: "We are not party to the existing hostilities, and have no intention to interfere in their political concourse, or gain a foot hold in their country. We go there to engage in trade, but under suitable guarantees for its protection. The extension of our commercial intercourse must be the work of individual enterprise. To this element of our national character we may safely leave it." *

This is typically self-congratulatory, and almost Nixonesque in flubbing over the main point. "We go there to engage in trade, but under suitable guarantees for its protection." What were those guarantees? Those guarantees were the unequal treaty system, which Chinese patriots of today excoriate in retrospect. The guarantees had been secured by British gunfire in two wars, and by French gunfire also. Our Secretary of State was making policy in a never-never land, assuming that the British empire would always carry on, that we would participate in its benefits, and that we were doing nothing of a power

* Cass to Reed, May 1957, cited in Stephen Chapman Lockwood, *Augustine Heard and Company, 1858–1862, American Merchants in China* (Cambridge, Massachusetts: Harvard University Press, 1971), p. 64.

politics nature ourselves, merely securing most-favored nation opportunities.

Again, here is Albert Heard, the merchant, writing to his senior partner in Boston, Augustine Heard, Sr., in 1860, after the British had achieved what they wanted in China: "You needn't be surprised if we become half English, living as we do under her protection, and witnesses to her great power in every emergency." * The Heards traded with the English in London, and they felt semi-British in Shanghai.

In short, the American government in the nineteenth century seldom had a consistently worked out political-diplomatic-strategic program in East Asia. The Perry mission to Japan in 1853–54, worked out by that eminent naval officer, did have a program, but after it succeeded in opening Japan, the British soon became the chief foreign power there. We did not have a national policy in East Asia that consisted of aims that might have to be backed by force. We never considered such action.

The weakness of our official establishment was an indication of this general attitude of neglect, of getting by with the minimum. We sent out our diplomatic envoys but relied on the local missionaries and merchants to do the work of representation, such as it was. The British consul sometimes had to lend his jail to the American consul, since the American consul didn't have one. Meanwhile back in Washington State Department expertise was not developed. Nelson T. Johnson, who became ambassador in the 1930's, was one of the first American diplomatic trainees in the Chinese language. The American Foreign Service for China was not really set up on a consistent

* Letter of September 4, 1860, cited in Lockwood, p. 65.

basis until 1924. The British had set up their China service in the 1840's.

I emphasize this point because many earnest historians have gone through the American archives and of course got an American story out of them. The achives do not lie. The myopia is with the historians. They find what the Secretary of State wrote, and they put some pieces together. Tyler Dennett, the leader of this flock, made his important contribution back in the 1920's. Ever since, we have had a tradition that there was an American China policy. I submit that in fact the American policy toward China in the nineteenth century was just a subbranch of British policy.

I remember being told by old China political scientist hands in the 1930's that toward Europe, we Americans had a policy of no alliances. Toward the Americas, we had the Monroe Doctrine. Toward China, we had the Open Door. That was our policy. Nothing about the treaty system privileges that we had enjoyed and were still enjoying, and that derived from someone else's active policy. The treaties didn't drop out of heaven. They came out of British guns.

Let us now look more closely at the Open Door. It has been decried as simply the cynical American move in the imperialism of 1898. It also has been praised as the American way of altruism and support of China, not seeking selfish advantage. No doubt it includes all these things. It is worth taking a moment to get the Open Door in perspective.

First we can see that there were two periods of nineteenth-century American expansionist or imperialistic sentiment. In the 1840's and 1850's, the period when

Perry went to Japan, the ideas of Manifest Destiny were prevalent in this country, as evidenced not only in the war with Mexico but also across the Pacific in a concern about the Far East. The Civil War and its aftermath, however, turned our national energies in other directions. It was only in the 1890's that the United States came to a second period of trying to keep up with the expansion of other powers in the Pacific. We did indeed keep up. The war with Spain over Cuba in 1898 was accompanied by separate moves taking over Hawaii and part of Samoa as island outposts in the Pacific, as well as the Philippines from Spain. Thus we gained a whole archipelago in the Far East in the same period when the imperialist powers of Europe in the years 1897 and 1898 were struggling to get their spheres of influence in different Chinese provinces.

In the background of this Open Door era were the strains in American society at the turn of the century. The end of the frontier had been announced in 1890. People had a feeling that the country had been filled up and that we must look overseas for more space for our trade and other activity. Urbanization had brought social disorder, and the many problems included strikes in which labor and capital were at logger heads. There was a nativist feeling in the country against further immigration. In this atmosphere, doctrines of imperialism were avidly discussed and propounded. The naval officer Captain Alfred Mahan talked about the necessity of naval power to hold bases that in turn could ensure the flow of trade. Theodore Roosevelt, both as a young political leader and as President, extolled our national vigor and the necessity to compete. Economists began to talk about the need for trading and investing abroad. Others were concerned about competing with world powers like the Russians and the British. Many had moralistic concerns, that we had a duty to mankind and must expand to help backward peoples in foreign places.

Americans generally feared the break up or partition of China, which was much talked about for two or three years and seemed to be in the cards from the end of 1897. This led us to consider the Open Door for trade in China, for a market and investment there. The Open Door, of course, had been a British idea from the beginning, a free trade idea. But in their competition with the Russians, the French, and the Germans, the British gave it up and began to develop their own sphere, the Yangtze valley. However, the Americans, and particularly John Hay, our minister in London before he became Secretary of State, picked up the Open Door idea, and he got help from William Rockhill, who had been in China as a diplomat, traveler, and scholar. Rockhill in turn got assistance and concrete ideas from a certain Englishman named Alfred Hippisley. I remember being introduced to this kindly old gentleman in London back in the 1930's. Dr. H. B. Morse, the historian of China's international relations, told me that he was a very historic figure, but as yet unknown to history. Only later did I find out that Mr. Hippisley was the man who gave Rockhill the specifics of the Open Door notes, which Rockhill then drafted for Hay. Hippisley was an English commissioner of Chinese Maritime Customs who had been assisting Sir Robert Hart in running the Customs Service for the Chinese government. The provisions of the Open Door notes, when they were put out in 1899, came straight out of the Chinese Maritime Customs, which was a representative, although rather independent, product of the British approach to China and essential for maintaining the treaty system.

The American Open Door notes asked, first, that the powers who were establishing spheres of influence in China not interfere with the vested interests of other powers within those spheres. Second, that everyone should agree that only the Chinese government could collect customs duties, according to the Chinese treaty tariff—in other words, maintain the treaty system. Third, that no preferential harbor dues or railroad charges should be allowed the subjects of a power with a sphere. In other terms, the Open Door notes in their first form were trying to counteract the sphere-of-interest approach of the Russian and German imperialists in China.

The Open Door idea expanded in 1900, because in the Boxer year the Russians took over Manchuria and there was a question whether they would leave. The second set of notes put out by Secretary of State Hay in 1900 talked about the administrative and territorial entity of China, the integrity of China. This phrase, the integrity or administrative entity of China, became a catchword, the implication of which was that the Americans supported Chinese nationalism, China's chance to develop as an independent nation. Out of this, then, came a two-headed idea. First, that we would seek me-too trade opportunities according to the treaty system that we had lived under so long in China. Second, that we were against the break up of China. We wanted it to remain a unified nation.

It may be observed that these notes were put out in the first instance in 1899 during an American election campaign. Mr. Hay seems to have been heading off extremists who wanted more action by the United States than he was willing to give. In other words, the Open Door must be seen from many angles, including that of American politics. It became a symbol. Business interests supported it because it seemed to promise opportunity for trade. Public opinion in general supported it as giving a chance to Chinese nationalists. This was indeed an altruistic and idealistic attitude, anti-imperialistic, which no doubt can be attributed partly to missionary thinking of the preceding generation. We have to accept the Open Door, therefore, as significant in the American mind, even though in fact it counted for very little in power politics.

It was cited thereafter every time anybody did anything in the Far East. When the Russians and the Japanese in 1907 and later decided to divide Manchuria, they quoted the Open Door in their public statements and then divided the area secretly. When an American Secretary of State took any steps about the Far East, early in the first paragraph he always had to maintain the Open Door. In fact, the Open Door was maintained by the British navy. The British navy, feeling weak as of 1902, joined up with the Japanese navy. The Anglo-Japanese alliance of 1902 to 1922 supported the Open Door—in other words, the continued treaty system. The Americans went along with that, letting others do the necessary, as they had done so often before. In 1922 the nine-power treaty on China ended the Anglo-Japanese alliance and committed all signers to preserve the Open Door in China, but with the means unspecified. Thereafter, we were up against the fact that we had no way to support this policy, though we still had the policy. In 1931 the Japanese moved into Manchuria and began to take over China. We invoked the Open Door, but we did nothing further. We had no way to do anything. But in the 1930's, Secretary Hull in particular used the closing of the Open Door as one of his major points of accusation against the Japanese.

Before trying to appraise American government policy toward China in World War II and later, let us look briefly at the American private participation in Chinese life in the unequal treaty or imperialist era. It was a place for traveling journalists, as well as for remittance men who were sent abroad by their families to keep them, for one reason or another, away from home. It was a place particularly for Americans working in private organizations, and these were sometimes big corporate bureaucracies. The Chinese Maritime Customs employees included some Americans, and there were others working for the Chinese government. Then there was an arm of the military, the Fifteenth Infantry, stationed after 1900 in Tientsin, besides a number of legation guards in Peking. Officers like Stilwell and Marshall passed through that channel in China. Quite separate were the mission boards and their bureaucracies, including the Christian colleges and their faculties. Another whole world consisted of the business firms—Socony and Texaco selling kerosene, the Asiatic Petroleum Company (a combine of Americans, British, and Dutch), the British-American Tobacco Company. Each of these big firms had branches and offices scattered over the country. In Shanghai the Americans had a particular interest in the Shanghai Light and Power Company. The Americans participated in the defense of Shanghai with their own national company in the Shanghai Volunteer Corps. Though the British dominated the Shanghai Municipal Council, this body also took account of the American component in Shanghai. The

American President Lines steamed into Shanghai; later Pan American Airways started a service there. Ten thousand Americans or so were involved in these enterprises, nearly all of them private in nature.

To facilitate their operations, we developed the China service within the United States Foreign Service, beginning in 1924. There was a language school under the legation in Peking. Scattered over China were some twenty consulates or other posts which formed an entire universe, just as China formed an entire universe. Members of the China service moved from one of these posts to another throughout their careers. A few would be assigned to some other country occasionally, but China service officers would ordinarily serve at as many as a dozen or fifteen different posts successively, all within the boundaries of China. Having got their basic training in the Peking Mandarin, they might have an experience in Manchuria, then in the southwest, then in Shanghai; they would see all aspects of the country, but they were essentially trained for the China service, just as others were trained for the Japan service.

The rest of the Americans, except for the military, were private individuals, and in varying degree all had an experience of participation in Chinese life. Without exception, it was the life of the upper class in China in which they participated, in other words, in the foreign treaty-based, privileged life that was associated with that of the Chinese upper class and to some extent intermingled with it. All these Americans, for instance, had servants. They were affluent compared with the masses of the Chinese common people. They had a chance to travel around the country. They went to summer resorts developed by foreigners in China—to Kuling in the lower Yangtze region or to Peitaiho north of Tientsin on the coast. These same summer resorts are favored by the Chinese Communist leadership of today. Like so much else, the summer resorts have been inherited. The missionaries picked them well.

Americans in China generally had a sense of security. Very few lost their lives except to disease. On the whole they didn't have unusually heavy responsibilities. At least they were not responsible for the country; they need not control it. There was no idea that they were in charge of it, as might have been the case with an outright colony. They simply were associated with the remaining Chinese upper-class elements in a rather peculiar treaty-privileged position. They would go back to the United States on furlough and then on retirement and add their impressions of China to the large American public sentiment about China. This is how, during several generations, a mystique of the China experience grew up in the United States.

This mystique or ideal image derived partly from the pleasures of life experienced by a common man who belonged to a theoretically egalitarian society but lived in a two-class country, where there was an upper class and a serving class or commoner class. The democratic American in this kind of life can remain at heart democratic. He is for the common man. But in practice he enjoys the service and the upper-class status, the special aura of being an American in a land with seething hordes of common people. It was very different from life in America, where you walked down the street as one of the people. In China you were a marked man. You might be nobody back home, in fact, maybe you were shipped out to get rid of you. But in China you were somebody. Socially speaking, you were highly visible, you stood out in a crowd. Legally you must be protected, the American flag cannot be lowered; if you got into trouble the consul had to come after you. You couldn't say, "I refuse my citizenship." The consul said, "No, you are an American citizen, so it is my duty to get you out of your trouble. We must preserve the system." It was all very pleasant.

Now this special situation was reinforced by the flow of returned Chinese students, who came to the United States for advanced training and then went back to China. This American-educated élite grew rapidly after the beginning of the century. In 1908 the Americans remitted to China part of their share of the Boxer indemnity, to be used for education in China and for sending students to the United States. A further remission in 1924 set up the China Foundation for the Promotion of Education and Culture. Something like 20,000 very competent, very able young Chinese came to this country to get their education and went back. At first they were used just as technical specialists, but after the 1911 Revolution they began to be the leaders of the new China—scientists, educators, administrators. The new Nationalist government at Nanking in the decade 1927 to 1937 boasted at one point that the majority of the cabinet were from Harvard.

The returned students became part of China's composite ruling class. Some may have had peasant or commoner origins, but most came from middle-class and more affluent or official backgrounds, from families with a tradition of education. When they came back to China, they were automatically part of the élite, not part of the peasant masses that were to be mobilized later by Mao Tse-tung and others.

Let us try for a moment to imagine the Chinese side of this situation. What impressions did the Chinese have of the Americans and what kind of experience? Many of those who had any contact at all needed American help. Sometimes they got jobs with American agencies. They found opportunity through American channels to get ahead, to get an education, even go abroad. In time of trouble they might get security in China through having American friends who could put in a word for them. This was a very mixed situation. The foreigner was in some ways better off than these Chinese, more privileged, more free of the political domination of a warlord or a corrupt official. For one thing the foreigner was probably better provided for materially. The Chinese who helped the Americans became, of course, a new wing of the upper class. The comprador, who handled the trade of the foreign merchant, became himself a merchant, a leading Chinese businessman or possibly a banker. The Chinese Christian pastor who worked with the missionary similarly became a leader in the Chinese Christian church.

Interpersonal relations were close. The tradition was illustrated again that the Chinese have had a great capacity, out of necessity, to take in foreign invaders, to collaborate with them, and eventually to neutralize them. The Chinese capacity for friendship, of course, was part of this. They and their American friends wound up with many common interests, many bonds of personal experience together, special relationships between Americans and Chinese.

Most of the private American experience in China

was without reference to national policy, and without reference to any responsibility that national policy might entail. The American government was a long way off, and until the 1920's, at least, the British and other people locally would do more than the Americans in policy matters. Out of this mainly private contact the American public got a series of stereotypes about China: First, there was the Young China of the 1911 Revolution, reformers and Westernizers. Then, unhappily, after that came the warlord period, when China was like a sheet of loose sand, unorganized and sunk in hopeless corruption. How could the Chinese ever get organized? Then there came the Nationalist government of the 1920's and 1930's. At first it was anti-imperialist and Chiang Kai-shek was known for a time as the "Red general." Then it turned anti-Bolshevik and anticommunist. From then on you could do business with the Nanking government. It maintained the treaty system. It was trying to build a noncommunist modern China. After 1931 this led into the period of the Japanese attack on its victim, Free China, which we supported first in sentiment, still shipping scrap iron and munitions to Japan; and then, after we stopped shipping those things, in sentiment and arms, in support of Free China in the war against totalitarianism.

Out of all this came an American public appreciation of the truly heroic qualities of the Chinese people. Think of Pearl Buck's *The Good Earth* and of Edgar Snow's *Red Star over China*. Think of United China Relief—many million Americans contributed to that in its time. Plainly the American public had many bonds with the Chinese people, whereas the American government was a different matter.

So we come to the question of American government policy after 1941. Pearl Harbor was the great
watershed. Before that time, the American contact with
China was mainly in private hands, through private corpo-
rations, mission boards, individuals. After 1941 it came to
be mainly in government channels. The American government was injected into the Chinese scene in a time of
warfare.

Now who was this American government? The policy makers included in Washington Dr. Stanley Hornbeck, with whom I seemed to have a good deal in common
since we were members of the same Greek letter frater-
nity, we had both been Rhodes scholars at Oxford, and we
had both taught at Harvard. In addition, Dr. Hornbeck
was certainly a China pundit who could pontificate on
what to do about China at the drop of a hat for several
pages in legalistic terms. He was, in short, a real bureauc-
rat, who signed as PAH, "Political Advisor Hornbeck," a
specialist put on top of the Far Eastern division of the
Department of State and whose signature was necessary
to its acts. So the whole Foreign Service staff in FE would
have to get Dr. Hornbeck to go along and lead the way. He
felt himself competing on behalf of China against the
more Europeanized and sophisticated parts of the Department or the Japan staff led by Joseph Grew and people
of like status, ambassadors from other parts of the world.
Dr. Hornbeck was an embattled pro-China hand who had
had experience there mainly as a teacher at Hangchow
before 1919 and had missed any contact with the May
Fourth Movement or the revolution.

The aid that we gave to China against Japan after
1941 turned out to be rather low priority. We went into the

war aware that we had to give priority to the war in Europe and get to Japan later. The United States Navy didn't get this message and went right ahead, but the high command in Washington pursued a Europe-first policy. So China became the end of the line. Things got there last, if there was anything left over, providing you could get it over the Hump, by flying it over the eastern end of the Himalayan range. In the end, China was bypassed, because the Navy got to Japan long before we could establish air bases in China to attack Japan from there.

Even before the war ended, we got involved in mediation between the Chinese Nationalist government and the Chinese Communists. At the end of 1945 General Marshall went to China for President Truman, and found himself in the peculiar position of trying to mediate even-handedly between the parties, although presumably the United States government could deal only with the accredited government of the country. In an earlier time private individuals would have dealt with anybody, government, nongovernment, rebel, or anything else. But during the war the United States government had been able to give aid and support only to the Nationalist government, to which its officers were accredited.

Our postwar policy was to urge reform to head off revolution, but the situation in China was too far developed. The civil war came as a contest between two organizations, one on the way out, worn down by all its burdens and problems, and one on the way in, with better ideas to meet China's problems and also better organization. The Americans by circumstance, through their governmental relations, were tied up with the old order, and therefore stood against revolution. We tried to wiggle out of this spot that history had put us in by constantly saying that we were mediating. But our arms were helping one side while we were mediating between the two sides. This is a very difficult stunt to get away with. The Chinese Communists negotiated for a while and decided we were really on the Nationalist side. I don't think we can blame them for that conclusion.

What had happened was that the American private participation in Chinese life, having gone on for a century or more, by the late 1940's had led to a division of sympathies. Many Americans had become sympathetic to the Chinese revolutionary effort, whereas others remained sympathetic to the Nationalist government. There developed a spectrum, a division of opinion, based mainly on the individual American's contact and experience. Meanwhile, quite contrary to this mixture of realistic private impressions and private attitudes stood an American government that had become involved in a war effort in China. It was now the main American presence on the scene, representing the American national interest, and this was not the same thing as private American interests. In supporting the Nationalist government, its wartime ally, it went against the Chinese popular interest, as it now turns out in retrospect.

I suggest that the American government—indeed, its whole policy-making process for China—suffered from a lack of national tradition or experience in defining the strategic power interests of the United States in China, and then defending those interests if necessary with force. We were getting into power politics without adequate preparation. We still said we didn't believe in power politics, even though we were in them up to our necks because we couldn't help it after World War II. The result was that we accepted our ideological anticommunism as an overriding, all-out necessity rather than bet, as the British did with greater insight and success, on the probability that China even when communist would remain a nation independent of Russia.

From our previous century of experience in China we were accustomed to enunciating a high level of rhetoric—abstract, moralistic, and righteous platitudes—without shouldering the responsibility of following up on them in action. As Chairman Mao might say, we had a gap between theory and practice. This, I suggest, lay behind the phenomenon that we saw in the Joe McCarthy era called "the loss of China." The loss of China, which we didn't possess, is a nonsense term unless one can understand the American mind at that time. It comprised a whole set of stereotypes. How many people there were who felt an interest in China, a commitment, an involvement. They had been there. Many of them were on the conservative side. They had worked with the Nationalists. Others, however, had been aware of the revolutionary movement and seen the Communists at work. But all of them had a feeling that China was an entity that concerned us. That's what they meant by the "loss of China." In other words, there was a very real psychological validity to that rather fatuous phrase.

The sense of loss was used, of course, to attack the Democrats in American politics, since American politics is our civilized substitute for violent domestic warfare. Anything goes, and the Republicans, who had been out of power so long under Roosevelt, felt that they could defeat little Mr. Truman, who wasn't always considerate of Republicans. But they found in 1948 that Mr. Truman—you recall that wonderful headline "Dewey Wins"—well, Mr. Truman won after all. That was a body blow. From that point on, after 1948, some Republicans were hysterical. Some became enraged over the "loss of China" as a conspiracy. Senator Joe McCarthy took advantage of the tension, suspicion, and antisubversive investigations of the time. The public obsession with possible conspiracy was not unlike the otherwise far different concern of 1974 over Watergate. New headlines everyday offered a new revelation from the investigation. (The ironic thing is that some of the people now in the headlines were at that time making the headlines.)

The unproven idea that the "loss of China" was brought about by a conspiracy engineered by "international communism" was fought off by a great many people, as best they could, and yet the overtones tended to capture them. In other words, the attitude of avoiding any suggestion of a procommunist posture crept into the State Department and the Congress and American public life. Joe McCarthy had his way with us, though really he was just a symptom of our incapacity, through ignorance, to understand and accept the Chinese revolution.

In the Cold War decades, we experienced a period of ideological crusading and anticommunist zeal. I suppose we might see it as emerging from World War II, because that war was a crusade against Nazi totalitarianism. Stalinism loomed as a further problem, a continuation of evil, so we kept right on going. In 1950, when we got into the Korean War, which seemed clearly thrust upon us, we militarized accordingly to fight in Korea. Somehow the stance of militant, crusading antitotalitarianism that had begun in World War II against the Nazis carried over into the Cold War period against Stalinism and lined us up against Communist China as part of the evil we must act against. The confrontation was by no means our creation only, for Communist China was just as much set against us ideologically. Even today this is not a simple problem on either side.

During the ideological Cold War we generally dismissed our old concern for the Chinese people, since they seemed to have turned against us. Meanwhile our firepower had increased more rapidly than our wisdom or experience. Besides our lack of experience in power politics—how and when to use force—we had never ourselves been bombed or invaded or occupied in defeat. We hadn't had the searing experiences that much of the world had had.

All these things lay behind the Vietnam chapter, which has not yet been closed. There were several stereotypes from our China history that influenced us concerning Vietnam—all the more because we were all so completely ignorant of Vietnam as a separate entity. One stereotype was that if you "lose" another East Asian country to communism, it will be political death for the party in power. The loss of China had been hung like an albatross around the neck of the Democratic party in a way that nobody in the party wanted to see repeated. This made for a take-no-chances, anticommunist approach to Vietnam, regardless of what was actually going on there. Again, we applied to Vietnam the stereotype of the Korean War: that there would be an invasion from the north and that aggression must again be stopped when this happened. But applying this to a civil war in the south proved a bit hard to handle. Instead of considering the specific historical forces at work in Vietnam, we substituted a simplistic ideology of fearing monolithic, atheistic, international communism, however unrealistic may have been such an attitude as a guide to policy or our true interest.

The Nixon rapprochement with Peking of 1972 was on the cards from 1960, when the Sino-Soviet split became apparent, because the Chinese-Russian-American relationship is a triangular one, and you can't expect two sides of a triangle to remain unconnected. As long as the Soviets had their contact with us and with Peking, we had to get in touch with Peking and vice-versa. Détente and negotiation, with a lower American posture, were certainly appropriate. China needed this opening toward the Americans, as they felt, to hold off the Russians, and so Mr. Nixon made his contribution.

This sudden outbreak of friendship produced a turnabout in the American attitude toward China. It came very quickly, paced by the reports of correspondents like James Reston of the *New York Times* when he got to Peking, had his appendix out, and received such friendly treatment. The whole aura of a China so mobilized, rational, and moralistic, and yet non-Western—in fact, so Chinese—hit him hard. He said that these people seemed engaged in a national barn raising, remaking their country with great enthusiasm. It seemed like old times in the USA of last century. The pleasure in exoticism, the admiration of Chinese virtues, the awe of Chinese achievements, were featured by all observers.

The Chinese, on their part, soon found that dealing with the American bourgeois craving for tourism was a problem. All kinds of Americans wanted suddenly to see

China. For the revolution, the old tourism would certainly be materialistic poison—rich foreigners asking questions and dropping money. Although unable to appreciate China's revolution from their own experience, Americans want the thrill of seeing China for its fabled differentness, just for pure excitement and out of curiosity. To study and understand the revolution, why revolution is necessary and how it is pursued in China, would take too much time. As an example, take the Canoe Project. There is a very eager and able canoeist in Cambridge, Massachusetts. His project, called Canoe, consists of getting to China with canoes and canoeing down the Yangtze. The Americans will be boys and girls, democratically selected. A Chinese counterpart group will also be selected, and they will get to know each other by canoeing together down the river, rapids and all, building the future through friendship. Incidentally, the Canoe Project will take color movies the whole length of the Yangtze River and put pictures in the *National Geographic Magazine.* If you look at this from a suspicious, security-minded Chinese point of view, it must seem not only nonproductive, foolhardy, and somewhat promiscuous, but straight out of the CIA —imperialist cultural aggression.

In sum, the time is past when China or "the Chinese" can properly be the object simply of our curiosity, our philanthropy, or our fear. Living with them in one world is going to be serious business, demanding study and effort on our part, not least because the tables have turned and we now seem to them out of date, backward, lacking in moral self-discipline and addicted to evils of affluent waste, individual license, and public violence that mankind can no longer afford to tolerate. At the same time, however, China's future is not ours. Neither our circumstances nor our traditions compel us toward their degree of collectivism and crowded living. Conflict and misunderstanding between us can be mitigated roughly in porportion as Americans and Chinese can see themselves and each other in a realistic historical perspective.

BIBLIOGRAPHICAL NOTE

The most recent scholarly survey of this neglected subject is by Warren I. Cohen, *America's Response to China: An Interpretative History of Sino-American Relations* (New York: John Wiley & Sons, 1971). A succinct and well-informed narrative, it also has a five-page bibliographical essay on recent items. J. K. Fairbank, *The United States and China* (Cambridge, Massachusetts: Harvard University Press, 1971), has an extensive bibliography on this subject on pages 475–482.

For a new look at the American opium trade see Jacques M. Downs, "American Merchants and the China Opium Trade, 1800–1840," *Business History Review,* XLII (Winter, 1968), 418–442; and "Fair Game: Exploitive Role-Myths and the American Opium Trade," *Pacific Historical Review,* XLI (May, 1972), 133–149. A close and illuminating view of missionary beginnings is in Edward V. Gulick, *Peter Parker and the Opening of China* (Cambridge, Massachusetts: Harvard University Press, 1973). Also Peter W. Fay, "The French Catholic Mission in China during the Opium War," *Modern Asian Studies*, *IV*, 2 (April, 1970), 115–128.

My own understanding of the missionary movement has been greatly enhanced by a dozen articles in a forthcoming volume, edited by me, *The Missionary Enterprise in China and America* (Cambridge, Massachusetts: Harvard University Press, 1974?). To associate myself in particular detail with the contributions in this volume would be ostentatiously parasitic; I have by no means done them justice in these lectures. Paul A. Cohen's chapter is on the "Christian Reformers," Philip West's on Yenching University.

On Christian education generally, I am chiefly indebted to the very solid work of Jessie Gregory Lutz, *China and the Christian Colleges, 1850–1950* (Ithaca, New York: Cornell University Press, 1971). I also had the opportunity of seeing half a dozen of them in action.

Out of the extensive literature on American China policy I am particularly indebted to work by Dorothy Borg, Kwang-Ching Liu, and Marilyn B. Young (including her *The Rhetoric of Empire: American China Policy, 1895–1901* (Cambridge, Massachusetts: Harvard University Press, 1968), among many others. For the latest reappraisal of the Open Door, see Michael H. Hunt, *Frontier Defense and the Open Door: Manchuria in Chinese-American Relations, 1895–1911* (New Haven, Connecticut: Yale University Press, 1973). However, the documentation of a lecturer's prejudices is a specious exercise too easily indulged in. These lectures derive from a repeated but incomplete pursuit of a many-faceted subject. Representing effort more than achievement, they may, I hope, provoke new work.

INDEX

United States anticom-
munism, 41, 72–77
Communist Party of China,
74, 75; Christian colleges
and, 32, 52, 53–54;
Nationalist government
and, 70, 72–73; summer resorts of, 67
Confucianism, 45; Christian
missionaries and, 21–22,
23, 54
Connecticut, 41
consuls, 24, 26, 28; merchant
services as, 57, 59; protec-
tive duties of, 68, 69
conversion; definition of,
40–41; advantages of, 69;
nationalist resistance to,
32, 52–53; numbers con-
verted by 1869, 24; revival
meetings, 50; social work
alternatives, 36, 37, 38, 39;
upper class resistance to,
22–23, 40, 54
Coolidge family, 16
cotton cloth, 34
Cuba, 61
cultures, 4, 7; China imprint
on Americans, 8–9, 67–68,
69–70, 77; 18th century
American values, 11–12;
19th century American
values, 15, 18, 19, 20, 22,
28, 29, 36, 37, 38, 40, 43, 44,
54, 61–62, 64; 20th century
American values, 74, 75–
76, 78–79; Western im-
print on China, 31–32, 33,
49–51, 53–54, 69, 77–78
Cunningham, Edward, 17
Cunningham family, 16, 57
Cushing, Caleb, 57
Cushing family, 16

Dartmouth College, 20, 43
defense, of China, 10, 25, 65.
See also armaments

Delano family, 16, 57
democracy, 11, 67
Democratic party (United
States), 74–75, 76
Denby, Charles, 57
Dennett, Tyler, 60
Dewey, Thomas E., 75
Dwight, Timothy, quoted, 20

East India 6, 7, 8, 10, 59, 76.
See also specific countries
East India Company, 14, 25
Edinburgh Conference
(1910), 51
education, 3, 20, 31–54, 55,
68–69; Confucian, 21, 22,
45; intercultural studies
and, 6–7
egalitarianism, 11, 27, 67
Emperor of China, The, 26
English language, 37, 40,
41–42; middle school
study of, 46, 49
Europe, 10, 11, 60, 61, 72. *See
also specific countries*
expansionism, 7, 60–61, 62;
American West, 12, 16, 17,
61
extraterritoriality, 26, 53, 55;
social effects of, 68

family planning, 3
famine relief, 46, 54
fan-shen, 53. *See also*
conversion
farm extension work, 46, 54
foot-binding, 22
Forbes, John Murray, 16
Forbes family, 16, 57
forestry schools, 46
France, 6; China trade
treaties of, 25, 26, 27, 58, 62
Free Enterprise doctrine, 7,
11, 12, 28; British Free
Trade doctrine and, 62, 64;
most-favored nation treaty
clauses and, 56, 58–59